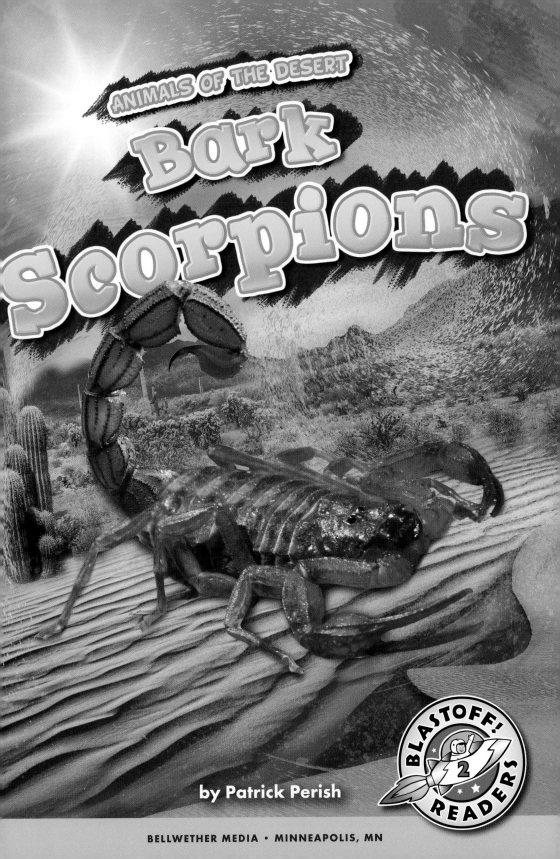

ANIMALS OF THE DESERT

Bark
Scorpions

by Patrick Perish

BELLWETHER MEDIA • MINNEAPOLIS, MN

Note to Librarians, Teachers, and Parents:

Blastoff! Readers are carefully developed by literacy experts and combine standards-based content with developmentally appropriate text.

Level 1 provides the most support through repetition of high-frequency words, light text, predictable sentence patterns, and strong visual support.

Level 2 offers early readers a bit more challenge through varied simple sentences, increased text load, and less repetition of high-frequency words.

Level 3 advances early-fluent readers toward fluency through increased text and concept load, less reliance on visuals, longer sentences, and more literary language.

Level 4 builds reading stamina by providing more text per page, increased use of punctuation, greater variation in sentence patterns, and increasingly challenging vocabulary.

Level 5 encourages children to move from "learning to read" to "reading to learn" by providing even more text, varied writing styles, and less familiar topics.

Whichever book is right for your reader, Blastoff! Readers are the perfect books to build confidence and encourage a love of reading that will last a lifetime!

This edition first published in 2019 by Bellwether Media, Inc.

No part of this publication may be reproduced in whole or in part without written permission of the publisher. For information regarding permission, write to Bellwether Media, Inc., Attention: Permissions Department, 6012 Blue Circle Drive, Minnetonka, MN 55343.

Library of Congress Cataloging-in-Publication Data

Names: Perish, Patrick, author.
Title: Bark Scorpions / by Patrick Perish.
Description: Minneapolis, MN : Bellwether Media, Inc., 2019. | Series:
   Blastoff! Readers. Animals of the Desert | Audience: Age 5-8. | Audience:
   K to Grade 3. | Includes bibliographical references and index.
Identifiers: LCCN 2018030994 (print) | LCCN 2018036921 (ebook) | ISBN
   9781681036304 (ebook) | ISBN 9781626179196 (hardcover : alk. paper)
Subjects: LCSH: Centruroides--Juvenile literature. | Desert animals--Juvenile literature.
Classification: LCC QL458.72.B8 (ebook) | LCC QL458.72.B8 P47 2019 (print) |
   DDC 591.754--dc23
LC record available at https://lccn.loc.gov/2018030994

Editor: Rebecca Sabelko   Designer: Josh Brink

Printed in the United States of America, North Mankato, MN

Table of Contents

Life in the Desert   4

Night Hunters   10

Pinching Prey   14

Glossary   22

To Learn More   23

Index   24

Life in the Desert

Bark scorpions live in deserts across the world. Many live in the American Southwest and northern Mexico.

This desert **biome** has wide-open lands dotted with brush.

Arizona Bark Scorpion Range

N
W E
S

range =

Deserts do not have much water. Bark scorpions are built to go long periods without water.

Waxy **exoskeletons** keep bark scorpions from drying out.

Bark scorpions are light brown. They are the same color as their desert homes.

This color helps them hide from **predators**.

Night Hunters

Bark scorpions have flat bodies.
They hide under rocks during
the hot day.

Then, they head out
to hunt at night.

Special Adaptations

body hairs

exoskeleton

flat body

Bark scorpions are one of the few types of scorpions that can climb!

They climb to find cool places to hide and wait for **prey**.

Pinching Prey

Bark scorpions **ambush** their prey.

They wait for prey to come to them. Body hairs help them feel when **insects** are near.

Bark scorpions' **pincers**
spring into action when
they feel an animal.
They grab their prey.

pincers

stinger

Powerful **venom** in the scorpions' **stingers** kills the animal quickly.

Bark scorpions get most of their water from their food.

They eat insects, spiders, and other scorpions!

Bark Scorpion Diet

cecropia silk moths

seven-spotted ladybugs

Turkestan cockroaches

Bark scorpions need very little **energy** to survive. They can live for months without much food.

These scorpions are made to live in the desert!

Arizona Bark Scorpion Stats

Least Concern	Near Threatened	Vulnerable	Endangered	Critically Endangered	Extinct in the Wild	Extinct

conservation status: unknown

life span: up to 6 years

Glossary

ambush—to hunt by lying in wait

biome—a large area with certain plants, animals, and weather

energy—the power to move and do things

exoskeletons—hard outer shells

insects—small animals with six legs and hard outer bodies; an insect's body is divided into three parts.

pincers—hooks at the end of a bark scorpion's body

predators—animals that hunt other animals for food

prey—animals that are hunted by other animals for food

stingers—sharp points at the end of bark scorpions' tails that are used to kill prey

venom—a poison created by a bark scorpion

To Learn More

AT THE LIBRARY

Davin, Rose. *Scorpions*. North Mankato, Minn.: Capstone Press, 2017.

Nugent, Samantha. *Scorpions*. New York, N.Y.: AV2 by Weigl, 2017.

Raum, Elizabeth. *Scorpions*. Mankato, Minn.: Amicus Ink, 2016.

ON THE WEB

FACTSURFER

Factsurfer.com gives you a safe, fun way to find more information.

1. Go to www.factsurfer.com.

2. Enter "bark scorpions" into the search box.

3. Click the "Surf" button and select your book cover to see a list of related web sites

With factsurfer.com, finding more information is just a click away.

Index

adaptations, 11

ambush, 14

American Southwest, 4

biome, 5

bodies, 10, 11

body hairs, 11, 15

climb, 12, 13

color, 8

day, 10

energy, 20

exoskeletons, 7, 11

food, 18, 19, 20

hide, 8, 10, 13

hunt, 11

insects, 15, 19

Mexico, 4

night, 11

pincers, 16

predators, 8

prey, 13, 14, 15, 16

range, 4, 5

rocks, 10

status, 21

stingers, 17

venom, 17

water, 6, 18

The images in this book are reproduced through the courtesy of: wacpan, front cover (tail); Jay Ondreicka, front cover (body), p. 4; Jon Manjeot, pp. 2-3; IrinaK, pp. 6, 9; Seth LaGrange, p. 7; Jared Hobbs/ SuperStock, p. 8; IrinaK p. 9; Rolf Nussbaumer/ AGEfotostock, p. 10; Hanjo Hellmann, p. 11 (inset); Michelle Gilders/ Alamy, p. 11; deepdesertphoto, p. 12; JB Manning, p. 13; Michael Francis Photography/ AGEfotostock, pp. 14, 16, 17, 18; Ed Reschke/ Getty Images, p. 15; Ilizia, p. 19 (top left); thatmacroguy, p. 19 (top left); Kucharski K. Kucharska, p. 19 (bottom); Fæ/ Wikipedia, p. 20; Jack Milchanowski/ Alamy, p. 21; DeepDesertPhoto/ Alamy, p. 23.